SHAC

7 Steps to Create & Step Into Your Vision

THE Audacity
TO RISE

THE AUDACITY TO RISE

ACKNOWLEDGEMENTS

There is just no way I could write any further without acknowledging the people in my life who have greatly impacted my growth and transformation. First, my parents, Joseph and Sandra Smiley. I love them both to the core, and appreciate the lessons that they have given me. I have the gift of writing and song from my father. My mom, she is the foundation on which I stood until I developed my own. Many nights she went on her knees to pray for me and my growing family as I struggled to find out how to play this game called life. She fought for me even when I did not know I needed to fight. The way she protected and covered me with my siblings was like no other. She introduced me to a higher power, and through Christ I discovered the power I had within myself.

Special thanks to my Aunties, Cynthia and Gerilyn, who were there for me at a fragile time in my life during my teenage years. I give thanks to my spiritual family, Mother Judy and Elder A. Williams. Elder A. Williams went on to be with the Lord, but was my father in Christ who encouraged me through my blind and arrogant rebellion. He had the patience of Job with me. Many times I could see the Lord through him and admired his caring, loving soul. He spoke raw truth that would tear you to pieces and then put you back together again. Mother Williams also treated me as her own child and spoke for me when I could not find the courage or words to say. She taught me along with my mother the power of prayer, at a time I did not know I would need it. I want to thank the mentors I have in my life that have inspired me to move passed my past.

A major company that has influenced my transition is, Dress for Success. I had no idea that coming through the doors and needing an interview suit would change my life and career path. There are so many such as, Joi Gordon, Ky Shabazz, Regina Norman, and Angela Williams, they all have been an instrumental part of my life in different ways and I thank them all for showing me the gifts I possessed. I thank the Lord for my children and allowing me to grow while being a parent in training. A special thanks to my cousin, Barbie Armstrong, who has been more like a sister and best friend rather than a cousin. She discovered my entrepreneurial potential as a teen and encouraged me to be empowered.

Thank you, Cousin Kia, for connecting me to Yolanda Brathwaite and her phenomenal women's group, Grown Girls. I am honored to be a member of professional women who support one another in love, life and in business. Andrenee Boothe, I know the Lord placed you in my life as I read, "Sacred Salutations." Your book and Facebook live posts motivated me to actually write the book I said I would do years ago.

Finally, to all of my family and friends. I love you and thank you for the part you have played in my journey.

TABLE OF CONTENTS

<u>FOREWORD</u>

This book, The Audacity to Rise: 7 Steps To Create and Step Into Your Vision, by Shaquan Hoke, is a short and powerful read. Her story is told with honesty as it leaps from the pages into your heart, pleading with you to believe in yourself and know that you were created for more than your circumstances.

Shaquan goes further and offers PRAYERS, a blueprint, a plan of action if you will, with actionable steps to assist in unleashing and discovering your purpose. Shaquan is passionate about sharing her experiences, challenges and growth, so that others can tap into their unique gifts and talents.

This book is a testimony of faith, self-discovery, and triumph. Shaquan's authenticity will encourage others.

I urge you to incorporate this book to your library.

---Regina Howard-Norman

<u>INTRODUCTION</u>

I hear many people complain about life and how it has impacted their ability to land a job. Huh?! So you think by being a good person with an easy life will help you solve your employment woos? I am so sorry to inform you that this is far from the truth.

Just so you know, don't think I fell from some sort of privileged family with a sizable inheritance. Here is a look into my side of the fence. I can assure you that once you have read my story you will see my point. There are just some things that will happen to you that you will have to either let it make you bitter or make you better. In the dark times of my life, I really did not know that I had a choice. I just allowed things to happen and tried to manage the best way I knew how. I only knew how to cope with problems by observing how my family coped with theirs. It was a rule for me to be seen and not heard, so I'm sure this did not do much for my problem solving and socialization skills. Needless to say, that as the eldest of two siblings without having someone to model after, I had a bumpy road ahead of me.

In this book you will learn the seven steps I took to create and move into my vision. After you read about my life story and the challenges I faced, you may see yourself or someone you know. If you do, it is ok to look back for a moment, just don't get stuck there. I will outline the seven steps in this book together with a basic plan on how to succeed on your next interview. I have used these steps over and over again and have gone from being a helpless, jobless single mother, to being a happily married, empowered entrepreneur with a career and now the Founder and CEO of Beyond A Job Inc., a career and employment consulting company that can be found on the web at www.beyondajob.net.

If I created and moved into my vision despite my past adversities, you can do it too!

MY GENESIS

In life, as with seeking employment, there are just some skills and qualifications needed at minimum to perform the job. Some employers expect you to already have these skills while others will train on the job. Earlier on, I knew I was not qualified for anything. I was told how I was never going to be good enough to have an education. My home would be life in the projects, and that I would have a family on welfare. That I would not amount to anything. Those words stung me to my soul, not because they were said, but it was who said it. Many did not believe in me. So how could I manage to rise above not only the cold world out there as well as in my own mind? Not to mention, while battling the demons in my mind, I tried burying myself under a pile of books and projects. How could I win the battle between me and the other side of me?

Before I dealt with myself and my own weaknesses, I began having relationships way before I was really ready. An example of this was a question I asked myself, but could not seem to answer for a long time. This question is rather deeply rooted in one's own soul, a question that will take several years to answer. So...what exactly is the question, you ask? "Why am I here?"

That is the four-word question that haunted me well into my thirties. You may ask me, "Why is this question so important or difficult?"

Well, here is my answer. There is no way I could see what I wanted to be when I grew up if I didn't know why I was even here on planet Earth. If you don't know what reason you have for being then how can you know what direction you will need to go? There is no easy way to get the best answer to this question as the person asking the question will have to go through a lot of trial and error first. In addition to trial and error, it will most definitely cost you time and money. Sometimes you will have plenty of both while other times you won't have enough of one or the other. Ever had money but no time to spend it? How about time but no money to spend? Well, I think you get the point.

Although it took me many years to really come up with the ability to discover my life, I could not just stand still. I kept moving in any direction that the wind would carry me. In public school, I knew that I enjoyed reading and writing. I loved to travel places and got to meet many characters through reading books. My mom would always yell at me about trying to sneak and read in the dark when I was supposed to be going to sleep. Once I started a book was a must for me to finish. I had to see what would happen next. It didn't matter if the book was for a school assignment or one I picked myself. I loved to connect with the characters. Often I tried to find myself in the story and would wonder if I would react the same way the characters did. Authors like Maya Angelo really resonated with me. Her poems and books like, "I know Why the Caged Bird Sings," was such a powerful story that I connected with. Through the story, I realized that I was her in so many ways. I could identify our similarities and differences, but noted how she never gave up. Although many things happened in her life, she didn't allow them to defeat her. I took many lessons from Maya Angelo. I kept moving and trying because I would allow myself no other way. I had to find myself or I would die.

THE FOUNDATION OF ME

I am a survivor. Most people really do not want to share the things that made them who they are today. Although in my past I have had many people look at me with judgmental eyes, that did not hold me back. So I know that you are waiting with baited breath to find out what have I survived. Where should I begin?

My mom did the best she could to raise three girls. Her husband was there and sometimes he took , "vacation," to sort things out for himself. I love both of my parents very much because each of them contributed to the person that I am today. Though I must say that without my mom being there by my side, even when I didn't want her to be there, I would not be alive today.

At a young age my family was always moving to different houses, often staying with relatives and close friends of my mom. During the times these events were happening, I could see how mom managed to keep a smile on her face despite the many changes she went through in her marriage. I remember seeing her at my school, in my classroom, and at Parent Teacher Association meetings. She was very active in my childhood, attending every event and show that I participated in. I was always into something as I have several things I enjoy.

Art allowed me to be creative and I drew from my imagination as well as what I saw. One of my drawings in public school was entered into a, "Say No To Drugs" contest and my drawing, was featured at the Brooklyn Children's Museum.

Another one of my favorite activities was poetry where my English teacher at that time named me, "Mystery," as my words were very impactful and mysterious in nature. In my childhood, I entered a poetry contest and came in third place in the world. My poem was featured in a book. The name of the poem is entitled, "Words." I remember this poem because in the poem I expressed how I felt when certain words were said to me or about me. I expressed how words can hurt deeper than a stab wound and that they can kill. In contrast, words can heal and give life to the receiver. This poem was created when I was a teenager. I guess you can say I may have been depressed during the time it was written.

A third favorite of my activities is music. I love to listen to and sing the words as a way to express my own feelings or the feelings of someone else I know. It's always been personal to me, so I began to write my own songs...just to have it. I remember singing every chance I had in church, talent shows, school, anywhere. I bet you can guess who was in the front row screaming, "That's my baby!" The way I physically expressed myself was with basketball.

8 | P a g e

I loved the competition and the challenge it gave me. I worked together with a team to achieve a goal but had my own talent that I was recognized for. I won a trophy for the team I played with. Unfortunately, after that mom pulled me off the team. Mom was afraid that the world would take advantage of me so anytime I excelled in sports or the arts she would take me out of the program.

There was always a dark cloud over my head, or at least that is the way I felt. I would get migraine headaches and have sensitivity to light, crowds and being affectionate. I also did not like being in confined spaces. Where did all of this come from? My mom knew that something was wrong with me and had me in church along with a psychiatrist to get help. I really did not know what was wrong either. All I knew is that I had knots in my stomach when in certain situations and needed to feel secure. It was not until my teenage years that the dreams I had and flashes of memory came together that I recalled being sexually abused. It doesn't matter who it was but the fact that it happened would not allow me to have the courage to tell my mother until I reached my twenties. I guess you could imagine how she took it, but she was always supportive and protective of me...even more so that I disclosed that information to her.

In my teens, boys began to take an interest in me and all I knew was that something was missing. I had this hole inside of me that I tried to fill. I loved seeing my dad when he was around and yearned for his approval. Sometimes I heard conversations that I should not have been privy to, but I was. As a result, I connected with people that as a teenager I was not ready to have intimate relationships with. I did not love myself. I tried to find what love was through my relationships. At the time, I did not realize that I only attracted the very things that I had inside of me. So I guess you can assume that things did not work out the way I thought they would. In my mid-teens, I began to create a family I was not prepared for emotionally, physically or financially. My family and friends really began to show me who they really were. Some were supportive and tried to connect me with resources to cover my lack. Others sat on the sidelines and shook their heads at me in shame, called me names and compared themselves to me and my deficiencies.

My first child was unexpected because it was the first time I had been voluntarily intimate and I thought it was love. I didn't listen to my parents as I felt they didn't understand me and wouldn't hear me. Boy, was I so wrong! He was like many teenagers trying to see how many notches he could get on his belt while me, the naïve one, had no clue. I did not get it until I surprised him one day after school; however, I was the one who was surprised. I saw him walking down the block with another girl on his arm. He spotted me and told me to wait while he had her stay up the block as he walked down to me. Of course, I asked, "Who was that?" and he dismissed her as just a friend like Biz Markie. I was so hurt because I knew he was lying to me but what was I to do?

A few weeks later, I discovered I was pregnant. All hell broke loose which put a further wedge between me and my dad. My mother was sad but she put on her supermom cape and protected me. She protected me from everyone who sought to attack me. I did not want to be protected though. I did not want to be here anymore. I just wanted to disappear. I wanted to die. One quiet afternoon in High School, there was no one in science class. The window was wide open and I felt so unwanted, so alone. I walked close to the window and asked God to help me. As I got to the edge, someone walked in the room and called my name. I was saved by the voice of the Lord that day. I cried horribly and no one knew that I was about to leap. No one saw the pain I had inside, the hole I had in my heart...no one but God.

The love I thought was love was not that at all, but later I learned that it was codependency. We were together from Junior High School, and at the age of 18, I had another child. For a brief moment I moved to Atlanta to be with my sweet grandmother who loved me and nurtured me as if I came out of her own womb. I moved there because I thought she needed me. I did not realize how much I needed her. She was patient with me and told me some things she went though. She shared things with me that made me see that I could get through this rough time in my life. In all things she told me to keep the Lord in my life. I witnessed how she took care of her grands and her home was a house of refuge.

Everyone knew my great grandmother for her kind giving heart and kind soul. She fed everyone that was hungry and would give her last. Some way or another she was blessed with what she gave out and then some. I witnessed this myself during my stay with her. I also saw some pain behind her eyes. I could see she went through a lot in her life. She fought for everything she had and still kept fighting to help others in need. I think this was the beginning of my awakening to knowing I was not here for myself. I was here for a purpose but I just didn't know what that purpose was.

Before I left Atlanta, I went into the field of being a Nurse's Aide for a year, and moved into my own apartment in Atlanta. My partner and I were supposed to be married, then I became pregnant with my third son. He took on two jobs to take care of us; however, the streets were calling him. He tried to find easy ways to make fast money. I noticed that he was in the street and it was becoming a danger to me and the children. I told my sister what was going on and she came to see me with a one way ticket back to New York. I went with her on a promise from him that he would stop running the streets, get himself together, come to New York and get us.

When I came back to New York, I stayed with an aunt for a while. He called me every day to see how we were doing and how he was planning his trip to New York to get us. Then one day there was no call. Knots formed in the pit of stomach. I couldn't sleep and when I did I dreamt of him being lost in a dark place. These dreams went on for a few days. As I dreamed, he couldn't see me and I couldn't see him but I knew he was there in a thick fog. Then on Christmas Day, I got a call from a detective saying that he was involved in an armed robbery. The detective continued to say that to avoid being captured he shot himself in the head. He was alive in the hospital for five days before he died in Savannah, Georgia. I guess you could imagine with me having two sons and a third on the way, the father of my two sons, my childhood companion, my fiancé was gone.

I needed help and then here came, Mr. GoodForRightNow. He fell in love with me and wanted to take care of me and my children. A year into the relationship I was pregnant. Well, into the eighth month I started getting strange phone calls. I found out that he was still legally married. I was so hurt and angry because of the omission of this truth, but I still tried to make it work. He kept saying he wanted to marry me but then said the lawyer said it was, "cheaper to keep her."

I asked him, "Just how long do you expect me to wait for you to get a divorce?"

There was never a reply. Later, he questioned his paternity to his son due to his strained relationship with his wife. So through the hurtful accusations I consented for a paternity test and it was concluded that he was the father. He apologized about a hundred times and asked me to give him another chance. In my mind it was already over. Although we were no longer together he took care of me and his son. He is a good person, just not the one for me. We are still on good terms to this day.

Finally, I had my own place and it felt good to put the key in my own door. Although I had children at a young age I knew that I had to grow up fast. I continued to put myself through school while working two jobs trying to finish my college education. I started out in law/paralegal studies to be exact. The world showed me that so many people were falsely accused of crimes that I felt compelled to be a help to the victims. At nine months pregnant with my fourth son I finished my associate degree in Paralegal Studies.

Two years later, and on birth control, I still managed to get pregnant again. Everyone kept saying that all I did was stay home all day, watch television and lay up. That was far from the truth, especially when I was in college and working two jobs. One job was to pay bills and the other was for the babysitter. I was depressed but I had no time to stop and feel. There was just too much going on and my children needed me to be a provider. That was all I knew how to do and I was not doing a great job at it.

CONQUERING MY GOLIATH

My life then took a turn for the worst two years later when I discovered I could not keep up with the rent on the income hike and the childcare expenses. In addition to all of this, I was pregnant again. This was my last one, I knew I couldn't have anymore. I lost my apartment and moved back in with my mom. I almost lost my daughter through the stress I endured. Although my mom was very supportive, I knew I could not stay in her home with my younger siblings. I felt like I would become a burden to her had I stayed with her. Also, my sisters were there and I did not want them to see me in the state that I put myself in. I had to leave and find a way to make it on my own with the family I created. Somehow, someway, I had to find my own way...

Things began to get tight and it became a bit much with me in the same house with everyone. I knew that although I was working full-time and in school, it was not enough to get another apartment. So I made one of the hardest decisions of my life. I decided to go into the shelter system. My mother had done enough as far as I was concerned and I did not want to be a burden, so I gathered everything I could manage to carry and went into the shelter with my five children ages six months through eight years old.

I will never forget my experience in the shelter system. There is a line for everything you needed to do and for the workers you had to interact with. There were questions on top of questions and I felt like I had committed a crime. The place for intake was horrible, unsanitary and unorganized. People from every walk of life were all around me and my babies so I kept them close at all times. The food was processed and packaged just enough to fill your stomach. I was so glad that I had money to buy healthy food for my children and was able to wash clothes.

The basic things that we take for granted like a clean bathroom, space, safety, and sanity, was there to remind me of what I had. Many nights I cried with no sleep and still had to work. I had to put college on hold as it was no way to comply with the rules of the shelter, go to work and school. After moving from several locations, we finally settled in one location and stayed for about a year. I continued to work and save money so that we could finally move. By the time they told me I may qualify for a housing program, I already had enough for furniture and to move out.

While working and preparing my exit from the shelter, I met my first husband. He was there for me from a few years before so he knew of the things I went through before I went into the shelter. I was able to bear the system knowing that I had someone I could talk to that would not judge me or my children. His mother and family accepted us as a family and helped in whatever way they could when we left. We had a lot of good years together and I am grateful for the lessons I learned about life, love and marriage. A few years later, we married. In total, we were together for ten years. Some good years and like most marriages towards the end we grew apart.

During my separation with my husband, I kept a two fulltime jobs as a Home Health Aide. I knew that this was not the path for me so I inquired about the Job Readiness Training with RDRC. This is a community center for residents in Far Rockaway in which I lived. Once I heard that they assist with employment, I immediately gave notice to both employers that I would be training. They thought I was crazy because this was a two week training and I would not have any pay. I also risked being fired from the jobs I worked but I felt in my spirit I was supposed to be there.

I treated this Job Readiness Training like a job. In the morning I arrived early before the instructors arrived and volunteered to help wherever it was needed most. The Job Developer took an interest in me and began to groom me for employment. I did not know that the very company I was training with had an eye on me. I was referred to Dress for Success for interview clothing and I was so amazed at the service they gave me. I knew I wanted to be a part of this company and began volunteering in the Queens Library to perform Job Readiness Workshops for Dress For Success. At the same time, RDRC hired me fulltime as a Case Manager. I no longer had to work two jobs and decided to use the time to go back to school. During my time, I transitioned from case management to facilitator, as the clients kept asking for me to come in the workshop. It was then I realized I could develop a curriculum for the Job Readiness Workshop since I was once a student. I saw what worked and what needed to be added to the lessons. So I began to have a triple role of facilitation, case manager, and assisting the Job Developer in getting jobs for the clients. The Job Developer gave me my start and showed me how to advance myself if I furthered my education. Although in the process of me growing into myself, my marriage was suffering and my children need my attention.

Towards the last years of our marriage he was distant. Although I went to try to get counseling he wasn't willing to participate. Sickness began to overtake me. One day at work, my eldest son came to visit me and as he sat at my desk, my face and the left side of my entire body got numb. The words were hard to come out of my mouth. My son asked me if I was ok and the next thing I knew I was sent to the emergency room. I had a TIA also known as mini stroke. My diet was horrible, I was not eating right, working two jobs and going to college to finish my Bachelor's Degree in Social Science. I was stressed, drained, and depressed but I felt like I had to keep going. Eventually, I was laid off due to lack of funding. Six weeks later, I was hired for the organization I was suited on for my first interview and volunteered with for two years. Dress for Success hired me and pointed out the strengths I possessed. I was challenged on many levels and that helped me to grow. Thankfully, I had a supervisor who also mentored me. She is still a part of my life today.

My husband at that time kept leaving and walking in a day later until one day he never came back. It was a hard time for me to deal with in addition to explaining it to my children. I know it was not easy for him either and he did what he thought was best. My daughter took it the worst. I sought to keep my family in church and also got counseling for my family. Time and prayer helped us all to get through. He is still a part of my children's lives as he supports financially and visits as often as he can. I appreciate that though we are no longer together, we can talk and laugh like normal beings do.

I took a semester here and there until I finally finished. My children saw how I struggled. They saw how I went from work to school. They saw me up late doing papers and rising early to do it all over again. It was my last semester of college that we separated. Although

I was torn up inside, I finished and brought home the cap, gown and the diploma. The proud look on my children's faces let me know that all that we went through together was worth it. The journey that I went through was not only for me, it was for them to see me press my way through. It was for them to see me overcome adversity. To have the audacity to finish college with five children. To have the audacity to overcome abuse, homelessness, depression, abandonment, and the statistics of a self-destructive black single mother. The audacity to not have all my sons in jail, on drugs or dead. The audacity to have smart, loving and caring children who believe in the good Lord and has values and ambition.

How did I manage to survive so many challenges at different stages in my life? I can assure you that it was not a simple process as some things took me years to learn. I will, however, give you the map that helped me along the way to not get stuck and defeated by outside forces or my inner demons.

In the next part of this book, you will find the seven steps to create your own vision. Hold on...not so fast. You can't just read about the seven steps though. There is some work that you have to put in as well. Don't worry, I have created some space for you to write, so you can work out the details that work best for you.

The acronym used for THE SEVEN STEPS TO CREATE AND MOVE INTO YOUR VISION is as follows:

P-R-A-Y-E-R-S

STEP ONE - PRAY

Pray (or meditate) and plan out the goals that you need to accomplish in detail. These goals need to be broken down by what you will do yearly, monthly and daily. For you to get started, you must write your goals down and review them daily. This will subconsciously keep your mind focused on the tasks that need to be completed.

DAILY GOALS:

1._____

_____

_____

2_____

_____

_____

3._____

_____

_____

4._____

_____

_____

5._____

_____

_____

MONTHLY GOALS:

1._____

_____

_____

2_____

_____

_____

3._____

_____

_____

4._____

_____

_____

5._____

_____

_____

YEAR END GOALS:

1._____

_____

_____

2_____

_____

_____

3._____

_____

_____

4._____

_____

_____

5._____

_____

_____

<u>STEP TWO – RECEIVE</u>

Receive the new day. Ok, so yesterday did not go as planned. So what! Get moving because today is a new day for you to focus on accomplishing your vision. Whatever you did not finish yesterday, add a little of bit it to today's task. What are you grateful for that you have accomplished to create your vision?

1._____
_____
_____
_____
_____
_____
_____

2._____
_____
_____
_____
_____
_____
_____

3._____
_____
_____
_____
_____
_____
_____
_____

4._____
_____
_____
_____
_____
_____
_____
_____

5._____
_____
_____
_____
_____
_____
_____
_____

STEP THREE – ACCEPTANCE

Accept that you have flaws and that things will not be perfect. Hey, even Superman has weaknesses right? He is a well-known superhero that is tasked with saving the world. Did you know that it is ok to make mistakes? Often times this is where the most important lessons are learned. Write down your flaws and what can you do to overcome them.

1._____

_____

_____

_____

_____

_____

_____

2._____

_____

_____

_____

_____

_____

_____

_____

3._____
_____
_____
_____
_____
_____
_____
_____

4._____
_____
_____
_____
_____
_____
_____
_____

5._____
_____
_____
_____
_____
_____
_____
_____

STEP FOUR – YELL

Yell at the top of your lungs the things you love about yourself. Do not skip this step as it may be the most important. How many times have people pointed out the flaws you have or the mistakes you have made? If you are not careful you may begin to say these things to yourself. Give yourself permission to love who you are NOW while you are creating and building the future you. What are the things you love about yourself? Write them down.

1._____
_____
_____
_____
_____
_____
_____

2._____
_____
_____
_____
_____
_____
_____

3._____
_____
_____
_____
_____
_____
_____
_____

4._____
_____
_____
_____
_____
_____
_____
_____

5._____
_____
_____
_____
_____
_____
_____
_____

STEP FIVE - EDUCATION

Educate yourself about the growing trends in your career field. This step is important for your current and future self. Are you in college now? Do you know if your field will be around and in demand 10, 20, or 30 years from now? You will want to do your homework on this to ensure that your career choice or business will sustain your quality of life in the future. No need to throw away money on something that won't be around for very long. Go to the Department of Labor in your neighborhood and speak to someone. You can also ask a career counselor at your college or the Small Business Association. Write down your options.

1._____

_____

_____

_____

_____

_____

2._____

_____

_____

_____

_____

_____

3._____
_____
_____
_____
_____
_____

4._____
_____
_____
_____
_____
_____

5._____
_____
_____
_____
_____
_____

STEP SIX – REVIEW & REVISE

Review your goals and revise them if needed. Some of your goals may have been accomplished, so maybe it's time to create some new ones. This is great because that means you are making progress. Other goals you have may require you to take more time to complete. All that means is you may need to break that goal down into smaller pieces and give yourself a new date to complete them. Write down the new or revised goals.

1._____
_____
_____
_____
_____
_____
_____
_____

2._____
_____
_____
_____
_____
_____
_____

34 | P a g e

3._____
_____
_____
_____
_____
_____
_____
_____

4._____
_____
_____
_____
_____
_____
_____

5._____
_____
_____
_____
_____
_____
_____

STEP SEVEN - STRATEGIZE

Strategize solutions for the problems that come into your life as they arise. Sometimes the the things we don't like to do, we tend to put them off. That can come back and bite you later on down the line. It is best to deal with the issues as soon as possible, so you won't feel like a heavy weight is looming over your head. What are some of these problems and how can you solve them?

1._____

_____

_____

_____

_____

_____

_____

2._____

_____

_____

_____

_____

_____

_____

3._____

_____

_____

_____

_____

_____

_____

_____

4._____

_____

_____

_____

_____

_____

_____

5._____

_____

_____

_____

_____

_____

_____

Now that you have gone through the seven steps: P-R-A-Y-E-R-S, you can begin to prepare for your business plan or interview. It is important to have all things taken care of like medical appointments, childcare, legal appointments, etc., before you start sending out your resume. There is nothing worse than to have an opportunity to interview, but lose it due to unpreparedness. In the following pages, you will see tips that can help you in preparing for interviews. These tips have helped me and many others transition from being unemployed to attaining a viable career.

CONCLUSION

I shared my story in the hopes to inspire you to move past the poverty mindset and into an upward momentum of motivation, independence and self-sufficiency. BEYOND A J.O.B. INC. was born out of the necessity to thrive in the face of adversity. I hope that you have taken in some of the lessons that I have learned to help me to create the vision I had for myself and to act on it.

There were many reasons for me to stay unemployed, uneducated and unmotivated. I realized that through the sevens steps of PRAYERS, that I had the power to change my situation. I no longer had to be unemployed and wait for a handout. I did not have to be at the mercy of a man or woman to help me take care of myself and family. I have the power to bring wealth, happiness, hope, education, peace and love into my life. Through the steps of PRAYERS I have furthered my education. I am now happily married to a man who enjoys seeing me create and be the entrepreneur that I am. I am healthy to date and have lost 50lbs through my wellness journey. My children are stronger and are growing into young men and a young woman who has a strong foundation through Christ and the power of PRAYERS. Life is not perfect but I certainly am not where I was back then.

I do not look like what I've been through and I thank the Lord for imparting PRAYERS into my life. You can use this to help you with your endeavors. If you use it you will become the best version of yourself. I see you...do you see you?

ABOUT THE AUTHOR

Shaquan Hoke, Founder and CEO of Beyond A J.O.B. Inc. - Career and Job Readiness Services, is an author, inspirational speaker, and training facilitator with over ten years of Professional Business Experience, Recruitment, Development, Sales and Job Readiness. Her company provides assistance in attaining the tools needed to gain employment or to map out a professional career, personal and business leadership coaching, inspirational speaking and leadership training to organizations across the world. Shaquan's focus is on the quality of service provided, not the quantity of clients served. She views her clients as dynamic and diverse individuals who have ever-changing life-demands and evolving goals. No matter what your aspirations may be, Shaquan believes you can address your personal goals with a customized plan tailored for your success.

Shaquan is currently completing her first solo book, "Beyond A Job: Seven Steps to Create & Move Into Your Vision"; which details her transition to true freedom through the application of Prayer.

Shaquan has facilitated workshops and professional trainings at Non Profits such as Dress for Success Worldwide, Women In Need, Easter Seals New York, The Boys and Girls Club, Brooklyn United and many more. Beyond A Job has proven success strategies and methodologies for career and employment services, effective communication, critical thinking, and understanding behaviors that support and maintain healthy relationships.

Shaquan walks in her divine purpose daily as a servant and leader to empower others to become the best person that they can be and ultimately fulfill their divine destiny in life.

For additional information visit website at
www.beyondajob.net

48156578R00031

Made in the USA
Middletown, DE
11 September 2017